Also by Evelyn McFarlane & James Saywell

If . . . (Questions for the Game of Life)
If² . . . (500 New Questions for the Game of Life)
If³ . . . (Questions for the Game of Love)
If . . . Questions for the Soul
How Far Will You Go?

If . . .

Questions for Parents

If...

Questions for Parents

Evelyn McFarlane & James Saywell
Illustrations by James Saywell

Villard/New York

Library of Congress Cataloging-in-Publication Data is available.

ISBN: 0-375-50283-1

Villard Books website address: www.villard.com

Printed in the United States of America on acid-free paper

9 8 7 6 5 4 3 2

First Edition

To parents everywhere
(the luckiest people in the world)

and to our own

If . . .

Questions for Parents

Parenting.

Can there be anything else in life quite as taxing, exhausting, confounding, complicated, surprising, frustrating, frightening, or unending? Or anything anywhere near as rewarding, fulfilling, enriching, intuitive, self-explanatory, revelatory, confirming, thrilling, unique, time-shortening, and wondrously joyous?

It is, of course, the most profound thing we will attempt to do in life, while also being, in a very real way, the most normal. Often it just happens, without great storms of doubt or insecurity or wrenching self-examination. Somehow we wake up one day and realize that there is another life in the house. One who will depend on us for everything, from their very survival to our own wisdom.

Anyone who has been a parent will have a thousand questions, most of them forgotten amid the rushed chaos of being a parent. They will also have 999 answers, usually learned from the child itself, perhaps indirectly, through a smile, a look in the eyes, the reaching hand of curiosity, the unprompted caress. Others, of course, will have been answered by experience.

These questions, our fifth collection in the *If . . .* series of books, are of another kind. The questions parents might ask, or be asked, to help dive into the imagination, and explore the treasure of thoughts, opinions, and ideas resting inside every person who is, has been, or dreams of becoming a parent. They are intended to prompt contemplation, shared recollections, surprising confessions, and unexpected laughter. In the end, perhaps, we hope they also remind us of the unequaled gift that children are: one bestowed on every parent, and entirely beyond the descriptive power of words.

If you were to name the best thing you could do for the eternal benefit of your child, what would it be?

If money were no object, how many kids would you want to have?

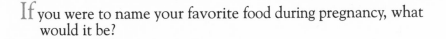

If you could prevent your child from inheriting one behavioral habit from your spouse and one from yourself, which would they be?

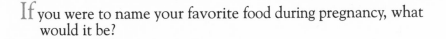

If you were to name your favorite food during pregnancy, what would it be?

If you had to identify what worried you most while pregnant, what would you say?

If you had to name the one thing you want more than anything else for your child, what would it be?

If you could have your kids do better than you in one area of life, what would you choose?

If you could know more about one area of your child's life, what would it be?

If you could determine the length of maternity leave employers had to provide, how long would it be?

If you could have your child's first word be anything other than "mama" or "papa," what would you pick?

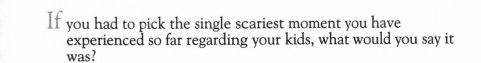

If you were asked whether you tend to teach your children to follow their hearts or their heads more, how would you respond?

If you had to pick the single scariest moment you have experienced so far regarding your kids, what would you say it was?

If you could afford to give your children one material thing right now, what would it be?

If you could purchase any gift for your child when they turn eighteen, what would it be?

If you could have your spouse contribute in one new way to raising your child, what would that be?

If you could change one aspect of your child's behavior, what would you alter, and how?

If you had to change one physical characteristic of your child, what would you change?

If you could spend more time with your child doing one specific thing, what would it be?

If you could have a heart-to-heart talk with your parents about one subject you have never discussed, what would it be?

If you named the one way you prepared for childbirth that was most valuable, what would you say?

If you were to select a single piece of advice from your own experience to give to someone who is now pregnant, what would you tell her?

If you were to choose someone famous to have a child with, who would it be?

If you had to have someone besides your mate in the delivery room, who would you want there with you?

If you were to adopt a child from one foreign country, which country would you prefer it to be?

If you had to identify the single biggest thing you fear for the future of your child, what would you say?

If something were to happen to you and your spouse, who would you want to raise your children?

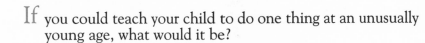

If you could teach your child to do one thing at an unusually young age, what would it be?

If you had to name the thing you dread most about your child's reaching adolescence, what would you say it is?

11

If you had to recommend one book to read while pregnant, which would it be?

If you were to determine the ideal amount of contact to have with your parents right now, how often would you see them?

If you had to identify one good and one bad aspect of behavior all your kids have in common, what would you say?

If you were to encourage your child toward one career, which would it be?

If you could learn the whole truth about one thing that happened to your child at school, what would you want to know about?

If there were a single thing about having a child that you could have someone else do for you, what would it be?

If you could alter your children's interaction among themselves in one way, what would you change?

If you could prevent your child from inheriting one of your physical characteristics, what would it be?

If you could go through pregnancy at the same time as one friend, who would you want it to be?

If your husband begged you to get pregnant with someone else because he was infertile, who would you choose to be the father?

If you had to name the one old wives' tale about childbirth that turned out to be the truest, what would it be?

If you were to choose the topic that is most divisive at family discussions, which would it be?

14

If you could have changed one thing about the care you received from your obstetrician, what would it have been?

If you were getting ready to explain the birds and the bees to your kids, how would you approach the task?

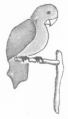

If you could ensure that your offspring learn one lesson about the issue of sex, what would it be?

If you were to determine the general policy on nudity in your house, what would it be?

15

If there were one adult you would prefer to keep distant from your children, who would that be?

If you could have your children do better in one subject at school, which would it be?

If you were to ask three questions to help a friend decide whether they really wanted kids, what would they be?

If you were to name the person you know who is best with children, who would win the honor?

16

If you had to describe in one word the role played by each family member in your household dynamics, how would you answer?

If you were to identify the biggest obstacle to communication in your family right now, what would it be?

If you were to name the three best books for youngsters, which would they be?

If one of your children admitted their own drug use for the first time, what would your reaction be?

If you had to name the person in your family who withdraws inward the fastest or most often, who would it be?

If you were to elect the person who is the most frequent scapegoat in your family, who would you say it is?

If you were to choose a member of your family to play peacekeeper, who would be the most logical choice?

If you could be more intuitive about one aspect of child raising, what would it be?

If you had to explain the concept of ethics to your kids, how would you approach it?

If one of your parents confessed to having a secret affair only to you, what would you say?

If you were to elect the person in your family who stirs things up the most when you all get together, who would it be?

If you were to name the one thing about your child's adolescence you most look forward to, what would you say it is?

If you had to say what you most look forward to regarding your child's entering adulthood, what would it be?

If you could have prevented your child from being friends with one person while growing up, who would it have been?

If you had to pick the most shocking thing you've ever seen your child do, what would you say it was?

If you had to remember the most shocking thing you've ever seen any child do, what would it be?

20

If you were to describe how personality differences among your family members complement and complete each other to make the family whole, what would you say?

If you were to identify the sweetest child (other than your own) you know of, who would it be?

If you had to give a prize to the most obnoxious television kid, who would win?

If you had to pick the best television role model for your kids, who would it be?

If you were to name the best television talk show or radio call-in show for parents you've ever seen or heard , what would you say?

If you were to remember the best Christmas you ever had as a child, which one would it be?

If you were to pick the best birthday you ever had as a child, which one would it be?

If you had to give one piece of advice to someone with kids about how to handle a divorce, what would you tell them?

22

If you were asked what the most difficult thing you ever had to explain to your children was, how would you answer?

If you had to repeat the wildest question your child ever asked, what would it be?

If you were to replace the ritual of baptism, what would you put in its place?

If you were to set a national policy on child circumcision for your country, what would it be?

If you had to name the worst ritual that we put children through, which would it be?

If you were to name the teacher of your children who most angered you, who would you choose?

If you had to name the worst single day of your own childhood, which would it be?

If you were to name the best single day of your own childhood, how would you respond?

If you were to guess the happiest moment in your child's life so far, what would you choose?

If you had to choose the age at which your child was happiest, when would you say it was?

If you had to choose the best name that friends of yours had picked for their child, what would it be?

If you now had to rename each of your children, what would you choose as replacement names?

If you had to pick the best and worst gifts your child has ever received, what would you say?

If you were to name the absolute best gift you ever received as a child, what would it be?

If you could totally redecorate your kid's room, how would you do it?

If you could share the thoughts and emotions of your child during one of their experiences in life, and know exactly what it felt like for them, which single experience (in the past or yet to come) would you choose?

If you could have your children experience your thoughts and emotions at any point of your life, when would it be?

If you had to pick the worst health scare that one of your children has ever had, what would it be?

If your child could be an exchange student in any country, where would you want them to go, and at what age?

If you had to pick the worst thing you've ever had to forgive your child for, what would it be?

27

If you had to think of the worst thing someone you know has forgiven their own child for, what would it be?

If you had to name the parents you know who are the worst at disciplining their children, who would they be?

If you had to name the one person you know who has the least ability to demonstrate their love for their children, who would it be?

If you could make one promise to your children that you are sure you could always keep, what would it be?

28

If you had to choose the cutest thing your child has done so far in life, what would you pick?

If your child confessed to you alone that they had committed a crime for which they might get life imprisonment or the death penalty if caught, what would you do?

If you were to choose the one career you would least like your child to pursue, what would it be?

If you had to come up with examples that best illustrate your children's personalities, what would you say?

If you could undo one thing your parents did, what would it be?

If you were to describe the one meal that most reminds you of home, what would the menu be?

If you could relive one of your childhood vacations, which would it be?

If you could go back and take revenge on one childhood bully, who would you pick on?

If you had to pick which baby-chore you most miss, what would it be?

If you were to choose which baby-chore you are most relieved you never have to do again, which would it be?

If you were to identify the most imaginative game your kids play, what would it be?

If you had to remember the worst trick you ever played on someone as a kid, what would it be?

31

If you had to admit to the most dangerous thing you ever did as a kid, what would it be?

If you were to choose the most dangerous thing one of your kids ever did, what would it be?

If you were to explain how to build trust between parents and children, how would you say that you had personally achieved it?

If you were to name the best and worst habits you had as a child, what would they be?

If you were to name the best moment of the day with your child, when would it be?

If you were to guess what the best moment of the day is for your child, what would you say?

If you had to pick the nicest tradition or habit your family had while you were growing up, what would it be?

If you were to name the dumbest tradition or habit your family had while you were growing up, one that you will not continue, what would you name?

If you had to recall the hardest thing that you ever told your parents, what would it be?

If you had to imagine what the hardest thing to tell your parents right now would be, what would you say?

If you were to think of what the most difficult thing to tell your kids would be, what would you say?

If you could ensure your child learned one moral lesson, what would it be?

If you were to teach your child the principle of tolerance with an example, how would you do it?

If you could show your kids one natural phenomenon in the world, what would you have them see?

If you could successfully instill three values above all others in your children, which would you want them to be?

If you were to teach kindergarten for one day, what would you do with the children?

35

If you had to explain the concept of nationalism to your child, what would you say?

If you could be a teacher, what grade and subjects would you prefer to teach?

If you were responsible for setting the salaries of teachers, how much would they be paid?

If you could force your city to provide one amenity for kids, what would you choose?

If you could change your nation's system of schooling, how would you do it?

If you could require one thing of all teachers, what would it be?

If you were to set the punishment for child abusers, how harsh would it be?

If you had to explain the meanings of love and hate to a child, how would you do it?

If you had to recall the best explanation of the facts of life you've ever heard, what would you say it was?

If you had to ask one person you know to explain the facts of life to your children, who would you choose?

If you could prevent your child from ever seeing one thing, what would it be?

If you were to pick the best kids' film ever made, what would take the honor?

38

If you were to declare what show on television is the worst one for children to see, which would it be?

If your son were drafted into a war neither of you believed in, what would you do to try to keep him out?

If your child became engaged to someone you *really* didn't like or approve of, what would you do?

If you truly believed your grown child was being taken advantage of by their lover, what would you do about it?

39

If your child's prospective employer asked you to say one thing to recommend them, what would you say?

If you were to send your kids to summer camp, what kind—and where—would it ideally be?

If you were to decide to make your child do one thing or have one experience against their wishes, for their own good, what would it be?

If you could send your child to the college of your choice, which would it be?

If you had to express one regret about child-rearing, what would it be?

If there were one thing you wish you'd done more or less of while raising your children, what would you say it was?

If you had to identify the thing that was most difficult for you to give permission to your children to do, what would it be?

If your child were asked to act in television and commercials, what conditions would you set, if any?

41

If you had to name the divorce you know of that had the worst effect on the children involved, what would you say?

If you were to name the divorce you know of that had the best effect on the kids involved, which would it be?

If you had to make the case for both nature and nurture by using the personalities of your kids as examples, what would you say?

If you could have back one thing from your own childhood home, what would it be?

If there were one thing that you had as a child that you'd love to have in your present home for your children's sake, what would it be?

If you were to volunteer to answer the phone for a youth crisis hot line, what would be the situation you'd most fear having to handle?

If you were to name the kids you know who have the worst and best eating habits, who would they be?

If you were to name the child you know who gets along best with their siblings, who would they be?

If you were to pick which year of child-rearing was easier than the rest, which would it be?

If you had to pick the year of child-rearing that was the most difficult, what would you say?

If you believe that love is blind, what about your children do you think you are most blind to?

If you were to identify the worst thing anyone you know has had to endure with regard to children, what would it be?

If you could move to another country to raise your kids, where would you want to go?

If you were to raise your family as part of another culture, which would you choose?

If you and your child could enter a children's story in real life, which would you pick?

If you could ask a children's author to write a story for *your* kids, which author would you choose?

If you could change the ending of one children's story, which story would it be, and how would you end it?

If Hollywood promised to make a children's movie from one book of your choice, which book would you want them to film?

If you could have one story for children made into a Broadway play, which tale would you want brought to life?

If you had to pick one animal that best represented your child's personality, what would it be?

If your child could have any pet they wanted, what do you think they'd choose?

If you had to name the one thing that would be hardest to take away from your child, what would it be?

If you were to name the moment you felt happiest while giving something to your kid, when would it have been?

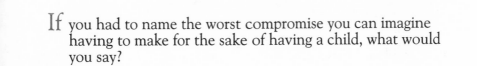

If you had to name the worst compromise you can imagine having to make for the sake of having a child, what would you say?

If you were to name the biggest compromise you actually did make in order to have kids, what would it be?

If you were to remember what the biggest surprise was about having kids, what would you say?

If you were to name the compromise you had to make to have children that was *less* difficult than expected, what would it be?

If you could describe the ideal school for each of your children, what would it be like?

If you were asked to describe your idea of the perfect teacher, how would you respond?

If you had to describe the ideal summer for your child, what would it be like?

If there were one thing you wish you hadn't said to your child, what would it be?

If there were one thing you wish your child had never seen, experienced, or heard, what would it be?

If you were to recall the most embarrassing thing your child ever did in public, what would it be?

If you were to describe the level of privacy you give your children, how would you do it?

If you were to describe the level of privacy your children deserve once they've reached puberty, how much would it be?

If your child wanted to bring a lover home to share their bed in your house, how would you react?

If you had to recommend how to teach teenagers responsibility, what would you say?

If you were to rate your liberality with teenagers, compared to other parents, on a scale of 1 to 5, where would you end up?

If you had to rate your hipness to youth culture, compared to that of other parents you know, how well would you do?

If you were to pick the all-time worst music or song your kids listen to, what would win?

If you were to choose the best music your kids ever introduced you to, what would it be?

If you had to pick the best movie, book, television show, or music video your kids ever introduced you to, what would it be?

If someone evil were trying to torment you by making you give up one thing for the sake of your children, what would be the worst thing they could choose?

If you had to choose the most ridiculous name someone you know gave their child, what would win?

52

If you were to identify one thing that you do with your children just to please your parents or in-laws, what would it be?

If you had to name the family member who most disapproves of something about the way you raise your kids, who would it be, and what would be their problem?

If you were to name the member of your extended family who was most supportive while you raised your children, who would it be?

If you were to devise a test that adults would have to take and pass before becoming parents, what would it entail?

If you had to name something that your child has done so far that has been underappreciated, what would it be?

If you were to pick the most well-adjusted kid you know, who would it be?

If you had to think of one characteristic that a person most needs to be a parent, what would you say?

If you were to name the weirdest thing your child loved to eat, what would it be?

If you were to give good reasons both for and against knowing the gender of your baby before birth, what would you say?

If you had to name the reasons for which you would consider aborting a child, what would they be?

If there were one thing about the changing modern world that frightens you for your children's sake, what would it be?

If you were to predict the most exciting prospect for your children's future world compared to your own, what would it be?

55

If you were to state the greatest historical event you have witnessed with your kids, and will always remember, what would it be?

If there were one still-living public figure who you'd propose as a role model for your children, who would take the honor?

If you were to describe what the idea of a "home" is to you, what would you say?

If you had to give a prize for the greatest invention for parenting, what would win?

If you were to cite the neatest thing your child has ever shown you on a computer, what would it be?

If you were to name the one ingredient that is most critical for your child's education, what would you say?

If there were something about being a grandparent that you look forward to, what would it be?

If you were to name the biggest way your parents have surprised you with regard to your own kids, what would it be?

57

If you were to think of one country or nationality that seems to have success with their methods of raising kids, which would it be?

If you asked your child to complete the phrase "The best thing about being a kid is . . . ," how would you expect them to finish it?

If you had to remember the nicest unprompted thing your child ever said to you, what would the magic words have been?

If you were asked to name your child's most truly irrational fear, what would you say it was?

58

If you had to predict what your child will be doing for each decade of their life, what would you say?

If you could prevent your children from falling into one of life's ruts, which would you want them to avoid, and how would you help help them do it?

If you could prearrange for your child to have three experiences in life, without being able to ensure how they would turn out, what would you pick for them?

If you were to adopt the child of someone you know, which kid would you take?

If you were to name someone you know who would most benefit from becoming a parent, who would it be?

If there were to be a new lullaby written expressly for your child, what famous singer would you want to record it?

If you were to state the most valuable thing you hope to leave your children, what would it be?

If you had to pick the greatest thing you've ever heard of someone inheriting from their parents other than money, what would it be?

If there were one family you know that is bringing up their children in a free-spirited way, which family would it be?

If there were one thing you'd most adamantly refuse your teenager, what would it be?

If you could be seven years old again for one whole day, knowing what you know now, how would you spend it?

If, as a parent, you had to state which trend in thought, public opinion, or values most disturbs you about your country, what would you say?

If you were to take your kids somewhere to teach them a moral lesson, where would you go, and for what lesson?

If you were to say you were building a safety net for your kids, what would that net consist of?

If you could warn your kids to watch out for *one* thing that represents insincerity, what would it be?

If you had to repeat the best response you've ever heard given to a child's question, what would it be, and who would have given it?

If you were to name a time in your family history when you think family counseling would have helped everyone, when would it have been?

If there were one person your kids should always listen to, other than their parents, who would it be?

If there were one person your children should never listen to, who would it be?

If you could teach your children how to deal with mistakes, or provide them with a philosophy for mistakes, how would you do it?

63

If your young child asked you what you think a person's individual obligation to society as a whole is, how would you answer?

If your young child asked you what "politics" is, how would you answer?

If a relative in the family died and you were forced to help your young child understand what that means, how would you go about it?

If you could teach one of your children something about their siblings to improve their relationship, what would it be?

64

If you could arrange for your child to meet one celebrity actor or sports figure, who would you pick?

If you had to identify the emotion that you most discourage your children from expressing, which would it be?

If you were to name the emotion that you most encourage your children to express, which would it be?

If you were to finish the phrase "My children respect me because . . . ," how would it read?

If you were to devise the fairest television policy for your household, what would it be?

If you had to hide something in the house from your kids, where would you put it?

If you were to recommend a way to teach kids that they can do anything they put their minds to, what would you say?

If there were one thing you'd rather not have seen in the delivery room, what would it be?

66

If there were one question you'd never ask your child, what would it be?

If there were one question you'd like to ask your child but haven't, what would it be?

If you were to name the one thing you'd most like your kids to say no to, what would you pick?

If your kids ran away from home, where is the first place you would look for them?

If you were going to teach your kids not to be afraid of the dark, how would you do it?

If you were going to teach small children how to deal with fear, how would you do it?

If you could use hypnosis to help your child with one thing, what would it be?

If you had to name one suspicion that would cause you to read your child's mail or search their room, what do you think it would be?

If you were to name the one thing you enjoy doing the most for your kids' friends, what would you say?

If you were to list the optimists and pessimists of the family, who would you list for each?

If you were to state one thing you are superstitious about with regard to your children, what would you say?

If you were to finish the phrase "The part of family life that I put the most work into is . . . ," how would it end?

If you had to give advice to your children on how to deal with bullies, what would you say?

If your child needed your advice to achieve popularity, what would you tell them?

If you had to give a child advice to help cope with rejection, what would it be?

If you could keep only one photo of your children, which would you hold on to?

If you could make one list to help your kids, what would be on it?

If you could ensure that your kids memorized one thing, what would it be?

If you could ensure that a pattern you have with your parents is not repeated with your own kids as you grow old, what pattern would that be?

If your kid were to be a prodigy in one field, what would you prefer it to be?

71

If your kid were a genius, what would you most fear for them?

If you had to predict one thing in the future that your children will have to forgive you personally for, what do you think it would be?

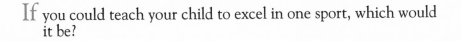

If you had to predict one thing in the future that your children will have to forgive your generation for, what do you think it would be?

If you could teach your child to excel in one sport, which would it be?

If you had to remember the funniest or most original excuse your child ever came up with, what would it be?

If you had to explain war to your young child, how would you do it?

If your child asked you what the three most important events of the twentieth century were, how would you answer?

If you had to teach the idea of "dedication" to your child, how would you go about it?

If you had to pick an effective way to teach kids the role of money in a good life, what would it be?

If you had to set allowance amounts for all children in every family in the country, how would you do it?

If it were up to you to decide at what age children should be allowed to get their first part-time job, when would it be?

If your child were offered a role in television, on what show would you prefer it to be?

If you overheard your child make a racist remark, how would you react?

If you heard someone else's child make a racist remark in your house or in your presence, what would your reaction be?

If your child asked you how they could change the world in one way during their lifetime, what answer would you offer them?

If you had to define for your child the reality of class difference in your society, how would you begin?

If you were to describe the absence from your children that was the most difficult to endure, what would you say?

If you had to cite the best trip you have ever taken without kids, which would it be?

If you were to guess how your child would answer the question "What's the worst thing about being a kid?," what would you say?

If you had to describe a moment in which you acted purely out of instinct regarding your children, what would it be?

If you were asked to write a national advice column for parents, what would be the subject of your first article?

If you were to name the single most affectionate parent you've known, who would it be?

If you were to pick the age at which kids are funniest, what would it be?

If you were to name the age most difficult for kids, what would you say?

If you were asked to pick the most eventful year in your child's life, what would you say?

If it were up to you to decide the age of consent for sex, what would you make it?

If you had to determine a minimum legal age of consent for producing a child, what would it be?

If you had to pick the ideal age for a child to leave home, what would it be?

If you had to name the most ambitious kid you ever met, who would you pick?

If you were to identify the most ambitious parents you ever met, who would they be?

If you were to choose a kid who most deserved the term "little devil," who would you name?

If you had to remember the moment at which you were angriest at your child, what would it be?

If you had to relate what caused your greatest anger at someone else's child, what would you say?

If you had to remember the time you made your own parents angriest, what would it be?

If you had to choose the dumbest pet children can have, what would it be?

If you were to name one aspect of raising a family that comes quite naturally to you, what would you choose?

If you were to give a medal for the most truly beautiful baby you've ever seen in real life, who (besides your own child) would win it?

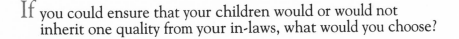

If you had to pick the least beautiful baby you've ever laid eyes on, whose baby would it be?

If you were to name the child who was most surprisingly transformed (in a physical sense) as they grew up, who would it be?

If you could ensure that your children would or would not inherit one quality from your in-laws, what would you choose?

If you had to pick the most helpful book for parents, which would it be?

If you could have learned one thing before you became a parent, what would it have been?

If you could give one criticism to another parent, what would you say, and to whom?

If you had to relate the single most insulting thing anyone has ever said to you about your children, what would it be?

If you had to predict when your relationship with your kids would shift from the role of a parent to one more like that of a friend, when do you think it would happen, and how?

If there were one thing your kids do that annoys other people but that you care little about, what would it be?

If you had to identify the least childproof aspect of your home, what would come first to mind?

If you had to name the single biggest change to your day-to-day life that parenting has brought, what would you say?

If you were to nominate the most child-friendly city you know, which would win the honor?

If there were a city you've been to where you would strongly avoid raising children, which would it be?

If you had to name one thing that seemed to bring instant comfort and calm to your baby, what would it be?

If you picked the nicest advantage of having daughters over sons, what would you cite?

If you were to name the best advantage of having sons rather than daughters, what would it be?

If you were to guess how much time you spend each week with your spouse discussing the raising of the family, how much would it be?

If you were to pick the greatest parenting day of your life, what would it be?

If you had to remember the worst parenting day of your life, what would you pick?

If you were to imitate the face your child makes that always makes you laugh, what would it look like?

If you were to mimic the most beautiful expression your child makes, how would it look?

If you were asked what you think your child's destiny is, how would you answer?

If there were one occasion when you think the Devil made mischief through your child, when would it have been?

If you had to cite the worst recurrent nightmare your kid has, or the worst one you had as a child, what would it be?

If you could have each of your children play a musical instrument, which would you pick for each?

If you were to name your first and most important duty as a parent, what would you say?

If you had to say one thing about the planet to your child, what would you tell them?

If you had to describe in complete, ruthless honesty what first went through your mind the first time you saw your newborn baby, what would you say?

If you could get your child to talk to you more freely about one thing in their life, what would you want to hear about?

If you were to pick the single feature of your child's face most similar to one of the parents', what feature would it be?

If you had to list three ideal qualities for fatherhood, what would they be?

If you were to choose the father you know in real life who is closest to ideal, other than your children's or your own, who would take the honor?

If you were to say that your family shares a common vision, what would it be?

If there were one fear you have about your children that you'd like to conquer, what would it be?

If your family were sent to live on a desert island for a year, and each of you could bring only one possession, what do you think each of your children would bring?

If you were asked to explain God to little children, how would you go about it?

If you could prevent your children from experiencing one single cause of sadness, what would it be?

If you were to name one aspect of child rearing in which you would like to emulate your parents, what would you say?

If you could discuss freely with one friend the subject of how to discipline kids, who would you pick, and what would you talk about?

90

If you were to name the biggest myth you previously believed about having a family, what would it be?

If you could be more assertive with your children in one area, what would it be?

If you were to recall the best and worst lessons a teacher at school taught your child, what would they be?

If you were to name a time when the body language of your child always speaks louder than their words, when would it be?

If you could have found out one thing about your parents sooner than you did, what would you have wanted to know?

If you were to name the ideal number of kids for a family to have, if money were no object, what would you say?

If you were to determine the ideal amount of time you would like to spend with your kids, how much would it be?

If you were to guess how many times a week you kiss your kids, what would your estimate be?

92

If you were to guess the average number of times you tell your children you love them, in a day, a week, or a month, what would it be?

If you were to pick the three best places to travel with kids on vacation, where would they be?

If you were to name the best kind of vacation to take with kids to stir their imaginations, what would it be?

If you could interest each of your children in something that now bores them, what would it be?

If you were to describe the most ridiculous outfit you have ever dressed your child in, what would you say?

If you were to recall the most embarrassing outfit your parents made you wear, what would you say?

If you were to pick the thing you do in front of your children that embarrasses them most, what would you say?

If you could compose the perfect family photograph, what would the details be?

If you were to say that you have brought "baggage" to your family relationships, what would those bags be?

If you could alter your children's eating habits, what would you change?

If you could change one thing about your kids' table manners, what would it be?

If you could have your child volunteer for any organization, which do you think would suit them best?

If you could have one law passed in your country to improve the lives of all children, what would it be?

If you were to describe what you think the special constitutional rights of kids should be, what would you say?

If you could go back and redo one incident that took place while disciplining your child, what would it be?

If you could change your home's design in one way to make it easier to raise the family in, what would you do?

If you were to name the best physical qualities your children got from you, what would they be?

If you were to name the time when disciplining your child hurt you most, what occasion would you describe?

If you were to name the smartest disciplinary action you ever took, what would it be?

If you could send your parents anywhere on a second honeymoon, where would you want them to go?

If you were to devise the ideal arrangement for the distribution of family chores, what would you propose?

If you could change one thing about the relationship between your spouse and children, what would you pick?

If you were to name the strongest thing about the relationship between your spouse and children, what would it be?

If you could undo one rule you set for the kids, what would it be?

If you could now set one rule for your children that you probably should have set earlier, what would it be?

If you had to name the one stepparent who was most able to fully integrate themselves into an existing family with children, who would it be?

If you were to make a ranked list of the things you spend the most time on, where would the family fall on that list?

If you were to make a ranked list of the things most important in your life, exactly where on the list would the family fit in?

If you were to name the time when each of your kids was most proud of themselves, when would it have been?

If you could naturally be more accepting of one thing your kids do, what would you like it to be?

If you were to name the thing you tend to boast about most when talking about your kids, what would it be?

If you could make each of your kids more independent in one area, what would it be?

100

If you were to recall the most painful thing your child has done or said to you, what would you choose?

If you were to recall the most hurtful thing you have done or said to your child, unintentionally or otherwise, what would it be?

If you had to predict what the political leanings of your children will be and who will most influence them, what would you say?

If you were to name the biggest turning points so far in your relationship with each of your kids, what would they be, and when would they have occurred?

101

If you were to describe how your relationship with your spouse changed most after the birth of your first child, what would you say?

If your child could pick one meal to eat every night for dinner, what menu would they choose?

If you were to prescribe the ideal interval of time between the birth of each child, what would you say?

If you could love one family member more than you do, who would it be?

102

If you could spend more time with one family member, who would you pick?

If you were to name the person in your family who needs your attention and time most, who would it be?

If you were to name the person in your family who gets most of your attention and time, who would it be?

If you were to name the family members that you worry about the most and the least, who would it be for each?

If you were to say in a word what the "family glue" in your household is, what would it be?

If you were to name the best moment during childbirth, what would it be?

If you were to guess how many hours a week your children watch television, what would you say, and would it please you?

If you could have any number and type of pets in the house, what would you have?

If you could get your baby-sitter to do one thing they do not normally do, what would you ask for?

If you were to recall the best party game for kids that you know of, which would it be?

If you could spend two hours a week as a family doing one thing that you do not currently have time for, how would you want to spend it?

If you were to state the biggest challenge you have met with so far in raising your kids, what would it be?

105

If you were to name the strongest mother and father role models you have had, other than your own parents, who would they be?

If you were to finish the phrase "I am qualified to be a parent because . . . ," how would you do it?

If you were to accept the idea that in the cycle of life, children pick up where their parents leave off, how would you fit in, relative to your parents and your own children?

If you were to name a shortfall in either of your parents' lives that you have fulfilled, what would it be?

106

If you were to name an area of failure in your own life that you hope your children will succeed in, what would it be?

If you were to say that your general outlook in life has changed since becoming a parent, how would you describe the difference?

If you had to determine the ideal age when a child should stop breast-feeding, what would you say?

If you had to name a common trend in child care that you disagree with, what would it be?

If your spouse had an affair today, and you separated tomorrow, what would you tell the children?

If you were to identify the toy that gave your child the most entertainment, which would you choose?

If you could keep one family secret a permanent secret from your kids, what would it be?

If you could bridge the generation gap between yourself and your children in just one area, which area would you pick?

If you were to describe one advantage to having a generation gap between yourself, your parents, and your children, what would you say?

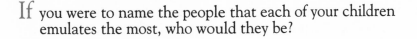

If you were to finish the phrase "The youth of today . . . ," what would you say?

If while you were pregnant you could take a pill ensuring that your child would be born with the IQ of a genius, with no side effects to you or the child, what would you choose to do?

If you were to name the people that each of your children emulates the most, who would they be?

109

If you were asked to name the one thing that makes your children happiest, what would it be?

If you were to finish the phrase "I am acting like my mother when I . . . ," how would it read?

If you were to finish the phrase "I am my father when I . . . ," what would you say?

If you could have changed one thing about the way your parents interacted with each other, what would it have been?

110

If you could have famous parents, what would you want them to be known for?

If you could have famous children, what would you want them to be known for?

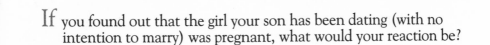

If you found out that one of your parents was gay, what would your reaction be?

If you found out that the girl your son has been dating (with no intention to marry) was pregnant, what would your reaction be?

111

If you discovered your child smoking at a young age, how would you react?

If you learned that your teenage child had a serious drinking problem, what would you do?

If your child wanted a tattoo at age thirteen, what would you say?

If your child wanted to pierce some parts of their body, what would you allow or disallow?

If you had to recall the time when your family laughed hardest and loudest together, what would you have been laughing about?

If you were to go to a sperm or egg bank to help conceive your child, what qualities would you request in the donor?

If you decided to have another child, but discovered that your spouse had only a year to live, what would you do?

If you were having trouble conceiving, to what lengths would you go to try to make it happen?

If your child failed to live up to your aspirations for their career and lifestyle, how do you think your relationship with them would differ?

If you knew that your children were guaranteed to be enormously successful as adults, how do you think your treatment of them now would differ?

If you were to name something that your child has done that makes you envious, what would it be?

If you were to devise the ideal arrangement for your children's inheritance, what would it entail?

If you could resolve one family feud that remains open, what would it be?

If you were to name the activity in the home that best stimulates children's imaginations, what would you say?

If you were to say that there was a right time and a wrong time to spoil a child, when would they be?

If you were to say that there was a right time and a wrong time to hit a child, when would they be?

If you were to identify the ways in which you treat girls differently than boys, what would you say?

If you could have your spouse be more like you in one area of raising the kids, and less like you in another, which areas would they be?

If you were to name the episode in your past that would be the hardest to talk to your kids about, what would it be?

If you found out that one of your adult children was posing for a pornographic magazine, what would you do?

116

If you had to decide the right time to tell a child they are adopted, when would it be?

If you could bestow the gift of immortality to only one member of your family, who would you give it to?

If you were to pick the age when a child should be allowed to set their own bedtime, what age would it be?

If you were to name the age when a child should be allowed to have a telephone or television in their own room, what age would it be?

If there were a time when you wish that, instead of intervening, you had let your child make a mistake for the sake of learning, when would it have been?

If you were to name a time when you wished you had intervened to prevent your child from making a mistake, when would it have been?

If you had to name a parent you know who is too domineering, who would it be?

If your child were asked to be in a talent show at school, what do you think they would do?

If you were to finish the phrase "A perfect child is . . . ," how would you end it?

If you had to give your best advice on potty training, what would you say?

If you could have a children's video that would help teach your kids one thing, what would you ask for?

If you could add any feature to your children's sneakers, what would it be?

If you could change one current fashion trend that your children follow, what would you alter?

If you had to name the dumbest thing you have to spend money on for the sake of your kids, what would it be?

If your child could receive a phone call tonight from anyone, who would you want to be on the other end of the line?

If you could have anyone show up at dinner tonight to surprise the kids, who would you want to come?

120

If you had to appear on a talk show tomorrow with your children, what would you tell the world about your family?

If you were to attend family counseling with one or more of your children, what issues would you work on first?

If you were to describe the perfect playmate for your child, what would their qualities be?

If you could have someone you know tutor your children at home, who would you want it to be?

If you could throw the ideal birthday party for your child, what would it include?

If you could program a new television channel for kids, what would it include?

If you were to name the kindest thing your child has done for someone else, what would it be?

If you could switch places with your children for one day, how would you act toward your new parents?

If you were to name the first lie you think your child told you, what would it be?

If you could eliminate the most offensive advertising campaign aimed at kids, which would you choose?

If you had to name one thing that your child is always getting in trouble for, what would it be?

If you had to name something that your child never gets in trouble for, what would it be?

123

If you could overhear your friends saying something about your kids, what would you most want them to say?

If your kids got together and collectively asked you to change one thing about yourself, what do you think they would request?

If you could put any prize in your kids' cereal box, what would it be?

If you were to predict which of your children will most likely take care of you in your old age, who would it be?

If you were to predict which of your children will live farthest from home, and which closest to home, what would you say?

If your child could do something today to make you instantly happy, what would it be?

If you could see one day in each of your children's futures, at which age would you like to see them?

If you were to cast a new sitcom based on your family, what actor would you choose for each family member?

125

If you could establish three new rules for the family that everyone, including parents, would have to follow, what would they be?

If you could start, or add to, a collection of any kind for your child, what would you collect?

If you were to predict the type of business that would suit each of your children best, what would you pick?

If you were to recall your worst baby-sitter experience, what would it be?

If you were to name the one family value that you and your spouse most disagree on, what would it be?

If you were to list the three most important questions to ask a baby-sitter before hiring them, what would they be?

If you could design a custom T-shirt for the family that would be meaningful for all of you, what would be on it?

If you could design a website for the family, what would it look like and do?

If your children could read your mind for a week, which of your thoughts do you think would most upset them?

If your children could read your mind, what thoughts do you think would make them happiest?

If you were to name the one thing that each of your children does that is most like a characteristic of the opposite sex, what would it be?

If you were to name the one thing that your child might do to their appearance that you dread most, what would it be?

If, God forbid, you were to lose one of your children, what single thing of theirs would you most want to keep as a memento?

If you had to prearrange marriages for all of your kids right now, with whom would you pair each of them up?

If you were to name the time when your kids saw you and your spouse at your happiest moment, when would it have been?

If you were to finish the sentence "The best thing about being a parent is . . . ," what would you say?

If you have an interesting or humorous question or answer to contribute to sequels of *If . . .* , we would love to hear from you. Please send your response or new question to the address below. Please give us your name and age, and sign and date your contribution. Thank you.

Evelyn McFarlane
James Saywell
c/o Villard Books
201 East 50th Street
New York, NY 10022

E-mail: author@ifbooks.com
Website: www.ifbooks.com

About the Authors

EVELYN MCFARLANE was born in Brooklyn and grew up in San Diego. She received a degree in architecture from Cornell University and has worked in New York and Boston as an architect. She now lives in Florence, Italy. In addition to writing, she lectures on architecture for the Elderhostel programs and is a full-time student at the Florence Academy of Art.

JAMES SAYWELL was born in Canada and lived in Asia as a child. Besides questions, he designs buildings and furniture. He divides his time among the United States, Italy, and Hong Kong.